2 Peter & Jude

30 Daily Insights from God's Word by **Eileen Poh**

Foreword

As I write this in the midst of the Covid-19 pandemic, so much of life as we know it has changed. Millions of people all over the world have been infected by the coronavirus, and many thousands have died. The future seems grim and uncertain. In these unprecedented times, we can look to 2 Peter and Jude for reassurance, guidance, and hope.

2 Peter begins with the marvellous reassurance that God "has given us everything we need for a godly life through our knowledge of him who called us by his own glory and goodness" (1:3). God has not left us to struggle with difficult experiences on our own.

Both Peter and Jude address the issue of false teaching, which is a problem in some of our churches today. While they expose the false teachers with their destructive heresies and fabricated stories, and the certain judgment that awaits them, Peter and Jude also give us practical guidance on how to deal with false teachers and those who are tempted to follow them.

Both authors also remind us of our Christian hope while we wait for the Day of the Lord. No matter what situation we may face in this life, we can all look forward to the new heaven and new earth that God has promised.

To Him "who is able to keep you from stumbling and to present you before his glorious presence without fault and with great joy—to the only God our Saviour be glory, majesty, power, and authority, through Jesus Christ our Lord, before all ages, now and for evermore!" (Jude 1:24–25).

Eileen Poh

We're glad you've decided to join us on a journey into a deeper relationship with Jesus Christ!

For over 50 years, we have been known for our daily Bible reading notes, *Our Daily Bread*. Many readers enjoy the pithy, inspiring, and relevant articles that point them to God and the wisdom and promises of His unchanging Word.

Building on the foundation of *Our Daily Bread*, we have developed this series to help believers spend time with God in His Word, book by book. We trust this daily meditation on God's Word will draw you into a closer relationship with Him through our Lord and Saviour, Jesus Christ.

How to use this resource

READ: This book is designed to be read alongside God's Word as you journey with Him. It offers explanatory notes to help you understand the Scriptures in fresh ways.

REFLECT: The questions are designed to help you respond to God and His Word, letting Him change you from the inside out.

RECORD: The space provided allows you to keep a diary of your journey as you record your thoughts and jot down your responses.

An Overview

Peter knew that he would die soon when he wrote the letter we now know as 2 Peter (1:13–14). In this farewell letter, he reminded his readers of what he had taught them in the past so that they would always remember his teachings after his death (v. 15). New Testament scholars believe it was addressed either to Christians living in the five Roman provinces in Asia Minor (1 Peter 1:1), or Christians in Asia Minor, Macedonia, or Greece, whom Paul had ministered to and who had also received Paul's letters (2 Peter 3:15–16). While most of Peter's audience were Gentiles, there would have been some Jews too.

The Structure of 2 Peter

1:1–11	Make every effort to grow in the knowledge of Christ
1:12–21	Know Christ from eyewitness accounts and Old Testament prophets
2:1–22	Be on your guard against false teachers who deny the sovereign Lord
3:1–13	Be on your guard against false teachers who deny the coming of the Lord
3:14–18	Grow in the grace and knowledge of Christ

The letter by Jude is a letter like 2 Peter. The author identifies himself as "a brother of James" (Jude 1:1). His letter shares a number of similarities with 2 Peter, including his warning against false teachers. Jude's readers were probably Jewish Christians who were familiar with the Jewish writings of the period between the Old and New Testaments (vv. 14–16).

Key Verse

His divine power has given us everything we need for a godly life through our knowledge of him who called us by his own glory and goodness. Through these he has given us his very great and precious promises, so that through them you may participate in the divine nature, having escaped the corruption in the world caused by evil desires. —2 Peter 1:3–4

Day 1

Read 2 Peter 1:1–2

Peter begins his letter by identifying himself and his readers (2 Peter 1:1), and he also includes his key theme, on which he will elaborate later.

Simon Peter was one of the Twelve, and was one of the leaders of the early church. Together with James and John, he was eyewitness to the Transfiguration (Mark 9:2–8), which he describes in 2 Peter 1:16–18. He identifies himself as "a servant and apostle of Jesus Christ" (2 Peter 1:1). Peter uses the term *doulos*, which is better translated as "slave" rather than "servant" in the NIV.

In the ancient world, a slave had no rights and was totally under his master's control. A slave had to submit to his master, or he would be punished. **Peter owed total allegiance to his master, the Lord Jesus Christ, and lived according to his master's bidding.** He was also an apostle of Jesus Christ: he was with Christ throughout His ministry and was eyewitness to His resurrection. These two designations affirm Peter's credentials as Christ's messenger.

Peter writes to "those who through the righteousness of our God and Saviour Jesus Christ have received a faith as precious as ours" (v. 1). While these words describe the readers, we must not miss the wonderful insights that Peter is sharing.

Firstly, the faith of Christians (that of Peter's readers in the first century and ours today) is a gift that we have received from God. Secondly, Peter assures his readers that their faith is "as precious as ours" (v. 1). This could imply that his readers are Gentile Christians, and that their faith is of equal value to those of Jewish background like Peter. It could also imply that the faith of his readers is not inferior to that of apostles like Peter. Peter probably has both in mind. Thirdly, this faith has come through "the righteousness of our God and Saviour Jesus Christ" (v. 1). This righteousness refers to Jesus' justice and impartiality, which ensures that our faith is as precious as that of the apostle Peter.

Peter ends his greetings with a blessing typical of other New Testament letters: "Grace and peace be yours" (v. 2). But what is untypical is the phrase "the knowledge of God and of Jesus our Lord" (v. 2), which is found only in this letter. Knowledge of God and Christ is a key theme of this letter (1:3, 5, 8, 16; 2:20–21; 3:17–18). By this, he means knowledge at conversion as well as knowledge which Christians acquire during their lives as disciples of Christ.

ThinkThrough

Think of the fact that your faith is of equal standing as that of the apostle Peter. How does that make you feel? How can this help you in times of difficulty?

Why is knowledge of God and of Jesus Christ so important in our Christian life? How can you know God and Jesus better?

Day 2

Read 2 Peter 1:3–4

When I was a younger Christian, I was afraid of straying away from God. I had heard stories of how some Christians had backslided, and I did not want to fall like them. I wish that someone had taught me about 2 Peter 1:3–4 then, because these verses tell us how we can live godly lives and not fall away.

Firstly, God has given us everything we need for life and godliness (2 Peter 1:3). This is so fundamental for Christian living and for resisting false teaching, that Peter dispenses with the usual thanksgiving clause found after the greetings in many other New Testament letters (for example, Romans 1:8, Ephesians 1:3, 1 Peter 1:3). Everything that is necessary for us to live godly lives comes from "his divine power" (2 Peter 1:3). Peter is referring to Christ's power, which He shares with God the Father. **Through Christ's divine power demonstrated in His life, death, and resurrection, we have been given everything we need to lead lives that please God** (v. 4).

This comes through our knowledge of Christ—a theme we saw yesterday. Peter stresses the need for Christians to grow in the knowledge of Jesus Christ. This knowledge came when we were converted, and grows as we walk in an intimate relationship with Christ. This is what Jesus has called us to. The "us" in verse 3 is not limited to Peter and the other apostles; it also refers to all whom Christ has called by His own glory and goodness. That includes you and me.

Secondly, we have been given "his very great and precious promises" (v. 4). The reason for this gift is that we may "participate in the divine nature" (v. 4). This participation does not make us gods. Rather, it refers to "those divine qualities that enable believers to escape the corruption in the world caused by evil desires".[1] In other words, by taking hold of the great and precious promises that God has given us, we can overcome sin caused by evil desires, both now and in the future.

God keeps His promises. By His grace, He has kept me from backsliding. He is able to keep us all from falling.

[1] Douglas J. Moo, *2 Peter, Jude* (Grand Rapids: Zondervan, 1996), p.43.

Reflect on the fact that Jesus Christ has given us everything we need to live godly lives. How can this help you to live a life that pleases God?

Read and reflect on some of these "great and precious promises" that enable you to resist sin: 1 Corinthians 10:13, Hebrews 4:14–16, 1 John 1:6–9.

Day 3

Read 2 Peter 1:5–7

If someone were to ask you, "What does a godly life look like?", how would you reply?

In 2 Peter 1:5–7, Peter paints a picture of a godly life with eight attributes: faith, goodness, knowledge, self-control, perseverance, godliness, mutual affection, and love. We are not automatically endowed with these virtues when we became Christians. Rather, we must "make every effort to add" (2 Peter 1:5) these virtues to our lives, though not strictly in the order listed in verses 5-7. (Peter is using a literary form common in his day for listing virtues or vices, which are not intended to be understood in the order they appear.)

Note that Peter begins his list with faith and ends with love (vv. 5, 7). We received faith when we first believed in Jesus as our Lord and Saviour (v. 1). As we walk in our Christian life, we must continue in faith.

Goodness is an attribute of God (vv. 3, 5). Peter borrows the word from the Greek world, where the word means "virtue" or "moral excellence".

We must add knowledge, which is the knowledge of God and of Jesus (vv. 2, 5), by reading and meditating on His Word daily. With this knowledge, we can discern God's will and align ourselves to obey Him.

We need to grow in self-control (v. 6) because it will keep us from giving in to temptations we face in our world.

Then we must have perseverance (v. 6), or steadfastness, to enable us to bear up under difficult situations.

Godliness (v. 6) is "a very practical awareness of God in every aspect of life".[2]

Christians must also have mutual affection for one another (v. 7), treating each other like members of one's family.

Peter ends the list with love, which holds all the other attributes together (see also Colossians 3:14).

This list may seem like a very tall order. But the good news is that we do not have to live a godly life by our own strength. Have you noticed the words, "For this very reason", at the beginning of 2 Peter 1:5? Peter wants to emphasise an important truth here, and that is: the attributes in verses 5–7 are linked to the preceding verses—God has already given us everything we need for a godly life (vv. 3–4).

[2] Michael Green, *2 Peter & Jude* (Leicester: IVP, 1987), p.79.

ThinkThrough

How would you know if you were living a godly life?

Which attributes in 2 Peter 1:5–7 are particularly challenging for you? Which ones do you have to "make every effort to add" (v. 5) in order to live a godly life?

Day 4

Read 2 Peter 1:8–9

For many years, I suffered from poor eyesight, which required me to wear contact lenses or spectacles with very thick lenses. Without them, I was almost blind. I could not see anything clearly, even when I held something very close to me.

Peter uses the analogy of near-sightedness and blindness to describe those who do not possess the qualities of a godly life (2 Peter 1:9). You might wonder: How can a person be both short-sighted and blind? Surely he can only be either? New Testament scholar Tom Wright's translation of verse 9 is helpful: "Someone who doesn't have these things, in fact, is so short-sighted as to be actually blind."[3] For Peter, those who believe that they lead godly lives and are not able to or refuse to see the true state of their Christian life, are "so short-sighted as to be actually blind"—much like the self-assured Christians in Laodicea whom Jesus describes as blind in Revelation 3:17.

Such people are not only blind but are also suffering from memory loss (v. 9): they have forgotten what it means to have been cleansed from their sins. We know from the rest of his letter that Peter is referring to the false teachers who have come into their midst.

But Christians who live godly lives are so different from the "short-sighted and blind". These Christians not only possess the attributes described in verses 5 to 7, but they also do so "in increasing measure" (v. 8). **When we continue to make every effort to add these attributes to our lives, we will be effective and fruitful in our knowledge of Jesus Christ** (v. 8). This will enable us to stand firm in our faith and not fall away. It will also make us fruitful and effective in our service to God.

Adding these attributes is like becoming clear-sighted again after having cataracts removed from our eyes and having new lenses implanted. They enable us to see clearly that God has forgiven our past sins and given us everything we need to lead godly lives. And we can eagerly anticipate the day when God will welcome us with open arms "into the eternal kingdom of our Lord and Saviour Jesus Christ" (v. 11).

[3] Tom Wright, *Early Christian Letters for Everyone: James, Peter, John and Judah* (London: SPCK, 2011), p.101.

ThinkThrough

How clear is your sight on the knowledge of Jesus and what He did for you?

How can you possess the qualities listed in 2 Peter 1:5–7 in "increasing measure"?

Day 5

Read 2 Peter 1:10–11

How can you be certain that you will not fall away from God but will be welcomed into His eternal kingdom? Some say it is God who will preserve us. Others say it is up to us to persevere. Let us consider what Peter says.

In 2 Peter 1:10, Peter urges his readers, whom he addresses as brothers and sisters, to "make every effort" to confirm their calling and election. Peter uses the same word in verse 5, where he had exhorted his readers to "make every effort" to live godly lives. This puts the onus on us. Yet our calling and election come solely from God (2 Peter 1:3; see Ephesians 1:4). **We know that it is by God's grace and initiative that He has called us and chosen us. But this must be confirmed or validated in the way we live our lives, and in the choices we make each day** (2 Peter 1:5–9).

Did you notice that 2 Peter 1:10 begins with "therefore"? This signals that Peter is bringing his opening section (vv. 3–9) to a close. In verses 3 to 4, Peter had assured us that God has given us everything we need to live godly lives. Relying on "his very great and precious promises" (v. 4), we can make every effort to possess the eight attributes in increasing measure, and we can confirm our calling and election. When we "do these things", Peter assures us that we will never stumble or fall away from God (v. 10).

For Peter's readers, this means that they must reject the false teachers and their denial of the sovereign Lord Jesus Christ who died for them and purchased them for God (2:1). When they persevere in this, then through God's grace they will be welcomed into the eternal kingdom of our Lord and Saviour Jesus Christ (1:11).

So is it up to God or up to us to ensure that we will not fall away from Him? Peter would say: "Both." On the one hand, it is God who has given us all the resources we need for a godly life, and He will preserve us in our faith. On the other hand, we must make every effort to live godly lives and persevere in our faith. New Testament scholar Douglas Moo puts it well when he writes: "God chooses us and ensures that we get to heaven. We need to choose God and live godly lives so that we can reach heaven."[4]

[4] Moo, *2 Peter, Jude*, p.60.

In what ways can you
confirm your calling
and election?

How does the
promise of "a rich
welcome into the
eternal kingdom
of our Lord and
Saviour Jesus Christ"
(2 Peter 1:11)
motivate you in your
walk with God?

Day 6

Read 2 Peter 1:12–15

As I grow older, I find that my memory is becoming more unreliable. Once, during a class on the Old Testament prophets, I asked my students to name the twelve minor prophets. They named eleven, but were not able to recall the twelfth. "Who is the twelfth, Eileen?" they asked. And at that moment, my mind went blank. I simply could not remember. It was most embarrassing!

We all need help to remember biblical truths that we have been taught. That is why Peter wrote his letter. He wants to "remind you of these things" (2 Peter 1:12), and "refresh your memory" (v. 13) so that "you will always be able to remember these things" (v. 15). By using "so" at the beginning of this section, Peter is linking "these things" in verse 12 to what he has just said in verses 3 to 11—that is, the need to live godly lives, thus confirming that they are true disciples of Jesus Christ.

It is not that his readers have completely forgotten what they had been taught. Peter acknowledges that they know and are firmly established in the truth (v. 12). But he is very much aware of the presence of false teachers in their midst, and he needs to remind them to continue to hold on to the truth so that they will not be swept away by "destructive heresies" and "fabricated stories" (2:1, 3).

Peter must have felt it imperative to remind his readers of the truths they had been taught. He knows that he is about to die soon (putting aside his metaphorical tent, 1:14), and will receive a rich welcome into Christ's eternal kingdom (v. 11). He hopes this last reminder will make a powerful impact on his readers.

Before Jesus left His disciples, He, too, knew that they would need reminding of the truths He had taught them. He promised that "the Advocate, the Holy Spirit, whom the Father will send in my name, will teach you all things and will remind you of everything I have said to you" (John 14:26).

We all have a tendency to forget. Forgetting one of the twelve minor prophets may be embarrassing but has no severe impact on my Christian life. But forgetting the fundamentals of our Christian faith and not living godly lives may cause us to stumble and stray away from God. We all need reminders; hence we need to read the Bible regularly, and we need to rely on the Holy Spirit to remind us of the biblical truths we have been taught.

ThinkThrough

What practices in church and in your life can help you remember biblical truths? For example, what truths does the Holy Communion, which Jesus established, remind you about? (See Luke 22:14–20; 1 Corinthians 11:23–26)

What practical steps can you take to help you remember God's Word? Think about some methods you use to remind yourself of other things, such as the main points of a sermon you have heard.

Day 7

Read 2 Peter 1:16–18

In 2017, the Collins Dictionary's chosen word of the year was "fake news". "Fake news" is misinformation and cleverly devised stories that seek to pass as legitimate news. In early 2018, the British government formed two teams to rebut false reports about the government on social media.

In 2 Peter 1:16–18, Peter is rebutting "fake news" that false teachers have been spreading about the second coming of Jesus Christ. He uses the word *parousia*, which is used 17 times in the New Testament to refer to Jesus' second coming. Peter states emphatically that he and the other apostles believe that Jesus Christ will come again (2 Peter 1:16). Their teachings are not "cleverly devised stories" (v. 16).

In his rebuttal, Peter tells of the time when he, together with John and James, saw Jesus transfigured before their very eyes (vv. 16–18, see also Matthew 17:1–8, Mark 9:2–8, Luke 9:28–36). Jesus had taken them up a high mountain where the appearance of His face was changed (Luke 9:29) and He shone like the sun (Matthew 17:2). His clothes became "dazzling white" (Mark 9:3), as "bright as a flash of lightning" (Luke 9:29). Peter speaks of Christ's "majesty" (2 Peter 1:16), which speaks of His divinity and glory.

The three of them had probably never seen anything like this before. And there was more to come. Peter and his friends saw Jesus talking to Moses and Elijah (Matthew 17:3)! Then a cloud came over them, and they heard a voice saying, "This is my Son, whom I love; with him I am well pleased" (v. 5).

Peter repeats these words in 2 Peter 1:17. He knows that it was God who spoke those words regarding His Son Jesus Christ. The words, "This is my Son", remind us of Psalm 2:7, which refers to the Lord's Son as the messianic King. The latter part of 2 Peter 1:17 ("with him I am well pleased") is most probably taken from Isaiah 42:1, which speaks of the Suffering Servant.

By recalling his eyewitness account of the Transfiguration, Peter wants to rebut false teaching about the coming of Jesus Christ. He reassures his readers that what he and the other apostles had taught them about the *parousia* were not cleverly devised myths that they made up. **They were eyewitnesses, and therefore they were competent to attest to the truth of what they had seen.**

The Transfiguration points to Christ's second coming. New Testament scholar Douglas Moo expresses this well: "The Transfiguration involves a transformation in Jesus' appearance, but it is a transformation that reveals his true nature. It is this glorious and majestic nature, hidden, as it were, during his earthly life, that will be revealed to all the world at the time of his return. Put simply, the Transfiguration reveals Jesus as the glorious King, and Peter was there to see it."[5]

[5] Moo, *2 Peter, Jude*, p.75.

What does the promise of Christ's return mean for you personally? How does it change the way you live now?

How can your life and actions reflect to others the truth and hope that Jesus will return?

Day 8

Read 2 Peter 1:19–21

have heard some people say: "We are New Testament Christians. We don't need to read the Old Testament." Peter would be the first to object to such thinking. He has already recounted his own eyewitness testimony to the Transfiguration to support his teaching and refute the charge that he and others are following "cleverly devised stories" (2 Peter 1:16–18). Now he turns to the Old Testament to reinforce his point.

Peter uses the term "prophetic message" (v. 19) to refer to the Old Testament in a general sense, and more specifically to Old Testament prophets. The prophets did not speak of their own volition: they did not utter their own words or their own interpretation of things (vv. 20–21). They did not suddenly say to themselves: "Right, I will write a prophecy after lunch today." Rather, they spoke the words which God gave them as they were inspired by the Holy Spirit. New Testament scholar Richard Bauckham puts it this way: "The Holy Spirit of God inspired not only the prophets' dreams and visions, but also their interpretations of them, so that when they spoke the prophecies recorded in Scripture they were spokesmen for God himself."[6]

Because of its divine origin, the prophetic message is completely reliable, and

Christians can depend on it (v. 19). And because of its divine origin, we must pay careful attention to the prophetic word. It is the light shining in a dark place (v. 19). Light is often used metaphorically to refer to God's Word. In Psalm 119:105, God's Word is "a lamp for my feet, a light on my path". When the day dawns, however, the light is no longer needed: this is when the "morning star", which refers to the Messiah (v. 19; see Numbers 24:17; Revelation 22:16), will come and establish His glorious reign in all the earth.

This was what the Old Testament prophets looked forward to, as did the early church. We, too, anticipate the glorious reign of our Messiah. In the meantime, we need the light of His Word—including the Old Testament—to help us negotiate the dark world in which we live.

[6] Richard J. Bauckham, *Jude-2 Peter* (Waco: Word, 1983), p.235.

Reflect on what
2 Timothy 3:16 says
about Scripture.
How are you study-
ing and applying
God's Word in
your life?

If God's Word is
light shining in a
dark place, how can
you use it to point
people to Jesus
Christ?

Day 9

Read 2 Peter 2:1–3

In some cities, you can see fake branded handbags and watches being sold in shops and markets. I have seen a photo of a stall displaying the sign: "Genuine Fake Watches"! Wearing a fake Rolex watch may not have drastic consequences, but other fake goods can have life-threatening consequences. Take counterfeit medicine, for example. Counterfeit pills are made and packed in such a way that they resemble the real articles. But they contain ingredients that can cause physical harm or even death. Being able to distinguish between genuine and fake medicine can be a matter of life and death.

It is just as crucial to distinguish between true and false teachers. In 2 Peter 2, the apostle turns his attention to false teachers and warns his readers about them. Just as there were false prophets in the Old Testament (in contrast to the true prophets who spoke God's Word in 2 Peter 1:20–21), there are also false teachers in the congregations Peter is addressing. Although he uses the future tense in 2:1–3, in other parts of his letter he uses the present tense (e.g. 2:12–14, 17–19). This tells us that he is not addressing a future problem, but a current one.

Peter draws a picture of the false teachers to help his readers identify them. Firstly, he exposes their *tactics*.

They are devious in presenting their false teaching (v. 1); they deny Jesus Christ as the One who paid the price to redeem them (v. 1); and they make up stories and do not teach the truth (v. 3).

Secondly, Peter spells out the *impact* of the false teachers in their midst. They are popular, and many people follow them because they like what they hear (v. 2). Their "destructive heresies" (v. 1) and immoral way of life will cause people to have a wrong concept of God and will give the Christian faith a bad name (v. 2).

Thirdly, he reveals their *motivation*: they do it for financial gain as they are motivated by their greed (v. 3).

Lastly, Peter is uncompromising about their *destiny* (v. 3). Only one thing awaits them: condemnation!

How can you tell whether a branded handbag or watch is genuine or fake? You put the item next to the real article, and you will be able to tell the difference. **There are false teachers in our midst today. We need to know God's Word so that we can distinguish between truth and false teachings.**

Why is it so important to reject teaching that denies the Sovereign Lord Jesus?

Whenever you read an article or hear teaching about Jesus Christ or the Bible, how do you discern truth from falsehood? What steps can you take to help you to be more discerning?

Day 10

Read 2 Peter 2:4–9

My husband and I use a prayer guide that focuses on Christians who face persecution and discrimination in different parts of the world. We pray for churches that are closed down by authorities, and for pastors and believers who are harassed or arrested, often on false charges. Sometimes, when I pray for these Christians, I wonder when God will deliver them from their suffering, and what He will do to their persecutors.

2 Peter 2:4–9 assures us that God will punish those who do evil and unrighteous deeds—the false teachers who teach "destructive heresies" (2 Peter 2:1) and tell "fabricated stories" (v. 3) that lead many people astray. These teachers are the wicked, who will be "held for judgment" (v. 4) and will certainly face judgment in the end (v. 9).

But we must not miss out on another important truth that Peter makes here: God knows how to rescue the godly (v. 9). To make these points, Peter looks to three examples in the past when God punished the wicked but delivered the godly.

In the first, God judged the angels who sinned against Him (v. 4). Even angels cannot escape God's judgment. Here Peter may be relying on a Jewish traditional interpretation of the account in Genesis 6:1–4, which holds that the sons of God—understood to be angels—were attracted to the daughters of men and married them. For this reason, God judged them.

The second example is God's judgment on ungodly people during Noah's day (v. 5; see Genesis 6:5–8:19). He sent the flood that destroyed all but Noah, his wife, and their three sons and their wives. God rescued Noah because he was "a righteous man, blameless among the people of his time, and he walked faithfully with God" (Genesis 6:9).

The third example is God's judgment on the cities of Sodom and Gomorrah for the wickedness of the people (2 Peter 2:6–8, see Genesis 19:1–25). Only the righteous—Lot and his family—were spared. Lot had chosen to live near Sodom after parting from his uncle, Abraham (Genesis 13:11–13). The people in Sodom sinned against God, and Lot had a difficult time living in a society where there was much depravity and wickedness. So God destroyed the cities of Sodom and Gomorrah, but rescued Lot.

Peter uses these three examples to encourage readers distressed by the false teachers in their midst. These teachers are teaching heresies and exploiting people, and it seems like God is not doing anything about it. But Peter reassures them: **God will rescue the godly from trials, and He will hold the ungodly for judgment.** This judgment may not come immediately, but it will surely come one day.

ThinkThrough

Are you facing discrimination or harassment because of your faith in Jesus Christ? How does 2 Peter 2:4–9 help you in such circumstances?

Spend some time praying for our Christian brothers and sisters who are suffering for Christ's sake in a country near you.

Day 11

In the film *Forrest Gump*, the main character Forrest Gump offers a box of chocolates to a woman sitting on a bench in the park, saying: "My mom always said life was like a box of chocolates. You never know what you're gonna get." Forrest Gump is using a simile, which is a figure of speech that compares two things. The use of similes—which usually use words such as "like" or "as"—can be a powerful literary device to make a point.

Peter uses a stark simile to describe the false teachers in 2 Peter 2:12—he likens them to "unreasoning animals". Animals are not rational creatures; they are ruled by their basic instincts. They have only one end: they are pursued, caught, and killed. Similarly, the false teachers do not act according to reason. In their audacity and conceit, they act in outrageous ways. They even mock the "celestial beings" who rebel against God (2 Peter 2:10). Even the angels who are agents of God's judgment against these rebellious beings do not treat these beings with contempt (v. 11).

Like animals, the false teachers can look forward to only one end: destruction. This is because they pursue the sinful desires of the flesh and indulge in their polluting lusts (vv. 13–14). They despise the authority of God and His Son Jesus Christ (v. 10). They are so conceited that they do not realise that what they are doing is wrong in God's sight.

These were some of the characteristics of the false teachers in Peter's day. There are false teachers in the church today, too. Knowing these characteristics can help us to identify them. **We must be on our guard and not be swayed by charismatic personalities or teachings that appear to be novel and sensational.**

What people say and how they behave will reveal who they really are. One way to test whether certain people are false teachers is to see whether their lives display the fruit of the Holy Spirit (Galatians 5:22–23) or the acts of the flesh (vv. 19–21). Are they arrogant and self-promoting? Do they engage in sinful lusts? Do they despise authority? Or are their lives marked by love, joy, peace, forbearance, kindness, goodness, faithfulness, gentleness, and self-control?

ThinkThrough

In Matthew 7:15–20, Jesus teaches His disciples to watch out for false prophets. How can you watch out for false teachers in your church or community?

What are some characteristics of false teachers today?

Day 12

Peter is not done yet with the false teachers. How else can they identify false teachers in their midst? In 2 Peter 2:13–16, he focuses on the sensuality and greed of the false teachers, whose appetite for sensuous pleasure is insatiable.

The pursuit of sensuous pleasure usually takes place under the cloak of darkness. But not for these false teachers: they are revelling in their pleasures in broad daylight (2 Peter 2:13)! They even indulge in their pleasures during the feasts (or fellowship meals) which the Christians hold during the day (v. 13). These feasts usually include the celebration of the Lord's Supper. No wonder Peter denounces them as "blots and blemishes" (v. 13). This is in contrast to the way Christians are to prepare themselves, to be found spotless and blameless before God when Christ comes again (3:14).

The eyes of the false teachers are "full of adultery" (2:14). They look upon every woman with lust, seeing each one as a potential adulteress. And they continue sinning and sinning. They are not able to stop because, as New Testament commentator Michael Green puts it, "lust is subject to the law of diminishing returns."[7] So their appetite for sensuous delight grows and manifests in even more depraved behaviour.

Not only are these false teachers gratifying themselves, but they are also seeking to seduce Christians who are not firmly established in their faith (v. 14). That is why these "unstable" believers are easy targets for the false teachers, who lure them into a trap, like hunters ensnaring their prey. And these false teachers do this for the sake of money.

Peter cites the story of Balaam in the Old Testament (v. 15). Balaam was a prophet who was offered a great deal of money by Balak, the king of Moab, to curse Israel (Numbers 22:1–20). On the way to Moab, Balaam was stopped when an angel of the Lord appeared before him. Ironically, Balaam was not able to see the angel but his donkey could (vv. 21–35). And the donkey spoke to him! God used a speaking donkey to restrain Balaam's madness (2 Peter 2:16). Like Balaam, the false teachers have wandered away from God's way to pursue their greed (v. 15).

How should we see these characteristics of the false teachers? I find New Testament scholar Tom Wright's exhortation helpful: "We ought to read this list, not with a self-righteous pride ('Oh, yes, look at those wicked people! Not at all like us!'), but with appropriate sorrow and fear. These tendencies are present in all of us; the point of self-control is to keep them back, to crucify wrong desires and grow right ones in their place."[8]

[7] Green, *2 Peter & Jude*, p.110.
[8] Wright, *Early Christian Letters for Everyone: James, Peter, John and Judah*, p.115.

Could you be an easy target for false teachers? How can you strengthen yourself against them?

How do you regard money? Is greed or love of money an issue that you struggle with? What can you do to "crucify wrong desires and grow right ones in their place"?

Day 13

Read 2 Peter 2:17–19

Some years ago, my husband and I decided to walk from Bradford-upon-Avon to Bath in England. It was a lovely spring day, and my husband reassured me that it was only 10 km. It was a very pleasant walk along the Avon River, but after we covered about 10 km, Bath was still nowhere in sight. We plodded on, and were most delighted when we spotted Bath in the distance. It turned out that the actual distance was 16 km! As soon as we arrived, we went to our favourite tea shop, where I drank a whole pot of tea.

Imagine how disappointed I would have been if the tea shop had not been serving tea that day! It would have been like the metaphor Peter uses in 2 Peter 2:17 to describe the false teachers. They are "springs without water". A thirsty traveller would be terribly disappointed to find a spring that has run dry. Similarly, the false teachers promise life through their teaching, but in reality they are not able to provide their followers with life-giving teaching, for they speak only "empty, boastful words" (2 Peter 2:18).

In verse 17, Peter also uses another metaphor to illustrate the same point. The false teachers are "mists driven by a storm". Instead of promising rain, the mists are, as New Testament scholar Richard Bauckham puts it, "the haze which heralds dry weather and is quickly dispersed by a gust of wind".[9] The false teachers promise their followers freedom from the fear of God's judgment, which allows them to throw away all moral restraint and live in any way they please.

But this is an empty promise. The false teachers themselves are not free. They are enslaved by their depraved lifestyle—carousing in broad daylight and revelling in their pleasures during the feasts, and they never stop sinning (vv. 13–14).

So, the false teachers' words may sound impressive, but in reality they are empty, arrogant, and deceitful. They appeal to "the lustful desires of the flesh" (v. 18), because that was the kind of life their target audience have just recently come out of. In 1 Peter 4:3, Peter describes their former way of life as one characterised by "debauchery, lust, drunkenness, orgies, carousing and detestable idolatry". They entice new Christians who are not yet grounded in the faith, are unstable (2 Peter 2:14), and can be easily seduced to return to the pagan ways that they had recently left. That is why Peter writes to warn believers of the false teachers by

exposing their true character and tactics. For these false teachers, divine judgment awaits.

⁹ Bauckham, *Jude-2 Peter*, p.274.

ThinkThrough

How can the descriptions in 2 Peter 2:17–19 help you identify false teachers?

How can new Christians be equipped to grow in their faith so that they will not be easy preys for false teachers?

Day 14

Read 2 Peter 2:20–22

When I was very young, my family lived in a village. My mother reared a few hens and ducks which she slaughtered for Chinese New Year. We had a rich uncle whose children wanted a piglet for a pet. So they bought a piglet and asked my mother to look after it. This piglet was kept in an enclosure, and my mother kept it very clean at all times. It was the cleanest pig in the whole village.

Of course, that is not the normal state of pigs. The proverb that Peter cites in 2 Peter 2:22 describes the true nature of pigs: "A sow that is washed returns to her wallowing in the mud." A sow which has been washed will not remain clean for long. It will return to the mud to roll in it again. Similarly, a dog will not walk away from its own vomit, but will go back to sniff around it (2 Peter 2:22).

These two proverbs describe the state of the false teachers. They had "escaped the corruption of the world by knowing our Lord and Saviour Jesus Christ" (v. 20); this describes their conversion, when their knowledge of Jesus Christ meant that they had escaped the corruption caused by evil desires (1:3–4). For these people to have known our Lord and Saviour Jesus Christ and the way of righteousness, and then to turn their back on Christ and all of Christ's

teachings, it will be worse than not having known Jesus (2:21). They are like the dog that returns to its vomit, and the sow that returns to wallow in the mud (v. 22).

This is a clear warning to the false teachers that their final judgment is certain. Peter has already spoken of their destiny: their condemnation hangs over them (v. 3), and swift destruction will come upon them (v. 1). They will be punished on the day of judgment (v. 9) and what awaits them is "blackest darkness" (v. 17). This is the destiny of these false teachers who knew Christ and His teachings but have turned their backs on Him and His grace.

This is also a warning to new Christians not to follow the false teachers, or they will come to the same end. **New believers must continue to grow in their knowledge of our Lord and Saviour Jesus Christ; they must take hold of God's promises so that they will not return to the corruption of the world from which they have escaped** (1:3–4).

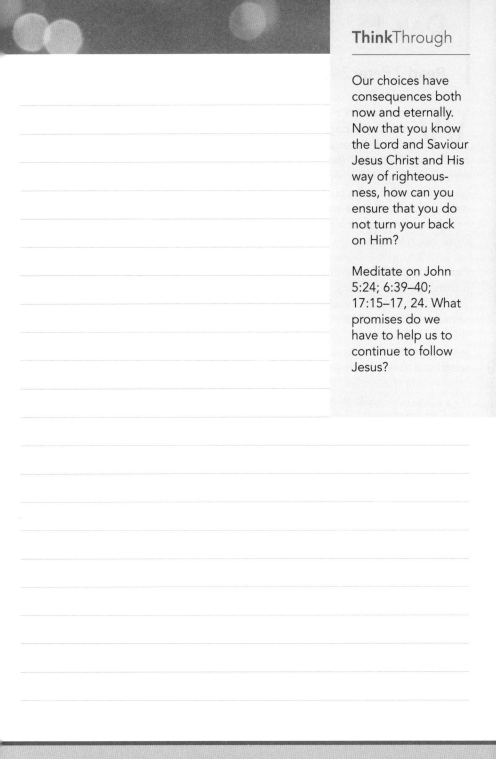

Our choices have consequences both now and eternally. Now that you know the Lord and Saviour Jesus Christ and His way of righteousness, how can you ensure that you do not turn your back on Him?

Meditate on John 5:24; 6:39–40; 17:15–17, 24. What promises do we have to help us to continue to follow Jesus?

Day 15

Read 2 Peter 3:1–2

We can detect a change of tone at the beginning of 2 Peter 3. Peter addresses his readers as "beloved" (NKJV)[10]. He refers to this letter as his second, but gives us no clue as to his first. We can only speculate that he was referring to 1 Peter, or another letter that has since been lost.

Peter's purpose for writing both letters, however, is very clear. He wants to remind his readers and stimulate them to "wholesome thinking" (2 Peter 3:1, see also 1:12–15). And he wants them to recall the teachings they had received from "the words spoken in the past by the holy prophets" (3:2), which refers to the Old Testament. They must also remember "the command given by our Lord and Saviour through your apostles" (v. 2, see also 2:21), which refers to the basic teaching of Christ as taught to them by the apostles. Peter wants his readers to remember these teachings so that they can counter the lies that the false teachers are propagating. These false teachers despise authority (2:10), but Peter refutes them with the authority of the Old Testament and the divine authority of the apostles.

The goal of recalling the Old Testament and Christ's teaching is for "wholesome thinking" (3:1). **Remembering God's Word is not a mental exercise nor an academic stimulation. Rather, it has to do with studying the Word and applying its truths to the situations and issues we face in our daily lives.** It is the direct opposite of what the false teachers do, which Peter likened to the depraved conduct of "unreasoning animals" (2:12).

We can recall God's Word by reading the Bible regularly and systematically, and meditating on how we can apply the truth to our daily lives. Another way to recall God's Word is to memorise Scripture and reflect on a verse or passage, to see how God wants to transform us through His Word.

[10] See also 3:8, 14, 17. While the NIV translates this as "dear friends", New Testament scholar Douglas Moo notes that it takes away something of the strength and Christian flavour of the original word *agapetoi*, meaning "beloved ones". It is the same word used in 1:17 when God spoke of his Son, "whom I love".

ThinkThrough

Take some time to review the way you study God's Word. How regularly do you read it? Do you read it hastily because you have pressing demands on your time? Do you find it easy to recall what you have read in your quiet time? Do you seek to apply God's Word in your situation?

Read Romans 12:2 and reflect on what Paul says about not conforming to the pattern of the world, and being transformed by the renewing of your mind. In what areas is your thinking conformed to the pattern of the world? How can you renew your mind daily?

Day 16

Read 2 Peter 3:3–4

Almost 2,000 years have passed since Jesus Christ predicted that He would return in glory one day (Matthew 24:36–39). The apostles in the early church taught about Jesus' second coming. But so many years have passed, and He still has not yet come. This may cause some to question or doubt New Testament teaching about the second coming of Jesus Christ.

Such a reaction is not new. Even in Peter's day, people were scoffing at the idea of Jesus' second coming and saying: "Where is this 'coming' he promised?" (2 Peter 3:4). Although Peter refers to such scoffers "in the last days" (v. 3), he is not referring to the end of the age. For the early Christians, the last days had arrived with the first coming of Jesus Christ. The last days as prophesied by the prophet Joel (Joel 2:28–32) were fulfilled when the Holy Spirit came upon the crowd listening to Peter on Pentecost (Acts 2:14–17). Hebrews 1:2 also notes that while God spoke through His prophets in the past, "in these last days he has spoken to us by his Son"—referring to the time when Jesus came to this earth. So when Peter speaks of "the last days" in 2 Peter 3:3, he is referring to his present day.

These scoffers argue that nothing has changed since their ancestors died (2 Peter 3:4)—referring to their ancestors in the Old Testament. They further argue that nothing has changed since the beginning of creation (v. 4)—that everything has gone on normally, and there has been no major event that has changed the world in a material sense.

We find scoffers today as well. Some may question or doubt the second coming of Jesus Christ, while others may scoff at the very idea of God. In October 2008, an atheist advertising campaign was launched in London with this message plastered on London buses: "There's probably no God. Now stop worrying and enjoy your life."

But these scoffers are mistaken. In the next few verses in 2 Peter 3, we will see how Peter refutes their arguments and explains why there is a delay in the second coming of Jesus Christ. **Just because there is a delay, he says, does not mean that the second coming of Jesus will not happen.**

ThinkThrough

"Jesus is coming again!" When was the last time you thought about the second coming of Jesus Christ? What emotions did you experience at that time?

How are you preparing for the second coming of Jesus Christ? What specific things are you doing?

Day 17

Read 2 Peter 3:5–7

You might have heard this trick question: "Have you stopped beating your wife?" If you say "yes", it means that you had been beating your wife in the past. If you answer "no", it means that you are still beating your wife. If you have never beaten your wife, you cannot answer this question, because it is based on a premise that is not true in your case.

The scoffers in 2 Peter 3:4–5 also base their argument on a false premise: that nothing has changed since the beginning of creation and nothing will change, so there will be no second coming of Jesus Christ. But this premise is false because there have been major changes in the natural world which the scoffers deliberately ignore.

First, Peter reminds them of creation (2 Peter 3:5). In Genesis 1:1–2, we read that: "In the beginning God created the heavens and the earth. Now the earth was formless and empty, darkness was over the surface of the deep, and the Spirit of God was hovering over the waters." By God's word, the water gathered to one place and dry ground appeared, forming seas and land (Genesis 1:9–10). **All this was done by God the Creator: He caused a major change in the natural world, a fact which the scoffers intentionally disregard.**

Secondly, Peter reminds them of how God destroyed the world through a massive flood in Noah's day (2 Peter 3:6; Genesis 6–8). As humankind was very sinful, God caused a great flood to destroy them. Only the righteous Noah and his family were kept safe in the ark that God commanded him to build.

God had caused these two past events of massive change in the natural world. Peter warns that the same God will bring about judgment and destruction on the heavens and the earth (which includes humankind) in the future (2 Peter 3:7), this time using fire instead of water. We will look at this in the next reading.

How might the fact that God the Creator is also God the Judge change the way you view Him?

God is also the God of history. New Testament scholar Douglas Moo says: "We need to recapture the biblical worldview, in which all of life is filled with the presence and activity of a personal, holy, and loving God, who is guiding history toward a definite end."[11] How does such a biblical worldview compare to your worldview?

[11] Moo, *2 Peter, Jude*, p.184.

Read 2 Peter 3:8–10

I met my husband Philip when I was doing my doctoral research at Tyndale House in Cambridge, UK, and we moved to Singapore a few years after our marriage. While in Cambridge, I was keen to visit the city of Norwich. Philip promised that he would take me there some day. Time and again, I would remind him of what I call his "Norwich promise". Eventually, after a couple of years, Philip kept his promise, and we went to Norwich and visited its lovely cathedral.

Delay in keeping a promise does not mean that the promise will never be fulfilled, or that the person who made the promise can no longer be trusted. This is Peter's point concerning the timing of Jesus' second coming. The false teachers have scoffed at their belief that Jesus will come again: "Where is this 'coming' he promised?" (2 Peter 3:4)

Peter reminds his readers that God's perspective of time is different from ours (v. 8), and refers them to Psalm 90:4. To God, a day is not 24 hours; a day is like a thousand years, and a thousand years are like a day. **We must follow God's timetable, not ours.**

Then Peter discloses God's delay for sending Jesus Christ a second time. It is not because He is slow or unwilling to keep His promise. Rather, it is because He does not want anyone to perish without Christ (v. 9); He desires everyone to repent and be saved. We might be impatient with a delay, but God is not like us. He is a patient and longsuffering God. If He delays in judging those who do not believe in Him, it shows His love for them.

But "the day of the Lord" will eventually come one day. And it will come suddenly and unannounced, like a thief burgling your house (v. 10). When that day comes, "the elements will be destroyed by fire, and the earth and everything done in it will be laid bare" (v. 10). While some older English translations of the Bible render the last part of verse 10 as "everything in it will be burned up", the more reliable manuscripts of this verse use a word that means "will be found", "will be discovered", or "will be disclosed".[12] When Jesus comes again to judge, the earth (which includes humankind) and everything done will be disclosed or laid bare before Him.

New Testament scholar Tom Wright explains it well: "What will happen is that some sort of 'fire', literal or metaphorical, will come upon the whole earth, not to destroy, but to test everything out, and to purify it by burning up everything that doesn't meet the test. The 'elements' that will be 'dissolved' are probably the parts of creation that are needed at the moment for light and heat, that is, the sun and the moon: according to Revelation 21 they will not be needed in the new creation. But Peter's concern throughout the letter is with the judgment of humans for what they have done, not with the non-human parts of the cosmos for their own sake."[13]

God will keep His promise. Jesus Christ will come again.

[12] Wright, *Early Christian Letters for Everyone: James, Peter, John and Judah,* p.119.
[13] Wright, *Early Christian Letters for Everyone: James, Peter, John and Judah,* p.119–120

How ready are you for Jesus' second coming? What areas in your life might you have to change as you prepare yourself for Jesus' coming?

God is delaying Jesus' second coming because He wants everyone to repent and believe in Him. How are you using this opportunity to share the gospel with those who do not know Jesus? Think of someone who needs to hear the gospel, and ask God for an opportunity to speak to this person about Jesus Christ.

Day 19

Read 2 Peter 3:11–13

suffer from migraine. Sometimes, the pain is so bad that I feel like banging my head against the wall. At times like these, I would say to my husband: "Can I have a new head?" Philip would remind me to look forward to the new heaven and new earth, where there will be no more pain (Revelation 21:4), and assure me that with my resurrected body, I will no longer suffer any migraine.

In 2 Peter 3:11–13, Peter encourages his readers to look forward to the new heaven and new earth that God had promised in the Old Testament (see also Isaiah 65:17, 66:22). He has just spoken about the heavens disappearing and the elements being destroyed by fire—possibly literal or metaphorical—on the day of the Lord (2 Peter 3:10). While reiterating this in verse 12, Peter also emphasises renewal in today's passage. On that day, God will fulfil His promise to bring about renewal to His creation by bringing about a new heaven and new earth (v. 13). The coming of Jesus will bring about both destruction and renewal.

In view of this, Peter asks, "What kind of people ought you to be?" (v. 11) Then he answers his own question: as we anticipate Jesus' coming, we ought to "live holy and godly lives" (v. 11). All that we do should reflect who God is; we are to be holy because our God is a holy God (1 Peter 1:15–16). **Our daily lives must be characterised by holy and godly conduct as we wait eagerly for His coming.**

Peter bases his exhortation on the anticipation of a new heaven and new earth, where righteousness dwells (2 Peter 3:13). By living holy and godly lives, Christians would be the kind of people who will be able to live in that renewed world. This is not a tall order, as Peter has already assured us that God's divine power has given us everything we need for a godly life (1:3).

Then Peter says something rather puzzling: that Christians can speed up the coming of Jesus (3:12). Is this not contradictory to our belief in the sovereignty of God? Doesn't God have His own timetable, and doesn't He alone know when Jesus will come again? Yes, but we have also learnt that God can delay the coming of Jesus because He does not want anyone to perish, but desires everyone to come to repentance (3:9). This repentance, from a human perspective, will hasten His coming. In New Testament scholar Richard Bauckham's words: "This does not detract from God's sovereignty in determining the time of the End, but means only that his sovereign

How often do you take into consideration the coming of Jesus when you make decisions in your daily life?

Read 1 Peter 1:13–16 and reflect on what Peter says about living holy lives. Is there a particular area in your life that you need to grow in holiness?

determination graciously takes human affairs into account."[14]

I still suffer from migraine. Each time I feel the pain, I am reminded to look forward to the new heaven and new earth.

[14] Bauckham, *Jude-2 Peter*, p.325.

Day 20

Read 2 Peter 3:14–16

Peter is now drawing his letter to a close. He ends with exhortations grounded in his readers' anticipation of the coming of Jesus Christ (2 Peter 3:14), and urges them to "make every effort to be found spotless, blameless and at peace with him". This echoes his earlier encouragement to his readers to "make every effort" to grow in Christian virtues (1:5).

For Peter, waiting for the coming of Jesus is not a time to do whatever they like with their lives or follow in the godless ways of the false teachers. Rather, it is a time to prepare themselves by living holy and godly lives (3:11) so that when Jesus comes, they will be found "spotless" and "blameless" in His sight (v. 14).

"Spotless" is often used to depict sacrifices that are acceptable in God's sight, with Peter describing Christ's sacrifice as "a lamb without blemish or spot" (1 Peter 1:19 ESV, see also Exodus 12:5). "Blameless" continues the sacrificial metaphor to stress that the sacrifice must be without blemish. Taken together, notes New Testament scholar Richard Bauckham, "the two words describe Christians as morally pure, metaphorically an unblemished sacrifice to God."[15] Christians are to be different from the false teachers who are described as "blots and blemishes" (2 Peter 2:13).

When Christ comes, Christians are to be found spotless and blameless in His sight (see Philippians 1:10, 2:15; 1 Thessalonians 3:13, 5:23). As we are waiting for that day to come, we may become impatient at times, and ask: "Why is God taking so long to fulfil His promise?"

Once again, Peter reminds us to see things from God's perspective. In 2 Peter 3:9, he had explained that any delay is due to God being patient with us and desiring all to repent and come to Him. In verse 15, he asserts that "our Lord's patience means salvation". **So there is still time for non-Christians to come to know Christ, and we must take every opportunity to share the gospel with them.** There is also time for Christians to repent from living for themselves, and to prepare for Jesus' coming by living holy and godly lives so that we will be found spotless and blameless on that day.

Peter then refers to Paul's letters which his readers had read (2 Peter 3:15). Is he referring specifically to "the Lord's patience means salvation"? If so, perhaps Peter has in mind a passage like Romans 2:1–9, which talks about God's judgment and mercy. Or is he referring more generally to Paul's teaching on ethics in view of the coming of Jesus? If this is the case, then he might have in mind passages like Romans 13:11–14, Philippians 2:15–16, and Colossians 3:4–6. I think it is probably the latter.

Peter concedes that Paul's letters are sometimes hard to understand and can be open to misuse by "ignorant and unstable people" who distort his words to their own destruction (2 Peter 3:16). Peter probably has in mind the false teachers he has been exposing in 2 Peter 2, and those who follow their wrong interpretation of Paul's letters and other Scripture.

Some of us may also find that Paul's letters or other parts of Scripture "contain some things that are hard to understand" (v. 16). While we want to understand God's Word, we must be wary of "ignorant and unstable people" who can distort Scripture for their own use.

[15] Bauckham, *Jude-2 Peter*, p.327.

If Jesus were to come tomorrow, would you be found "spotless, blameless" in His sight (2 Peter 3:14)? What changes do you need to make in order to be ready for His coming?

How can you avoid being like "ignorant and unstable" people (2 Peter 3:16) who misinterpret God's Word?

Day 21

Read 2 Peter 3:17–18

More than 20 years ago, I led a group of students on a mission trip to a town in Malaysia. On our way there in a bus, we passed through various towns and villages. After some time, a Japanese student asked: "We have passed the sign 'AWAS' so many times. When are we going to arrive in AWAS?" He had thought that "AWAS" was the name of a town. I explained to him that "AWAS" meant "caution" in Malay; the sign is a warning for motorists to be careful when they drive.

Not knowing warning signs can be a dangerous thing. Peter knows that, and so, in the last two verses of his letter, he reiterates his warning against false teachers (2 Peter 3:17). He urges his readers to be "on your guard" so that they will not succumb to these teachers' "fabricated stories" and "empty, boastful words" that promise freedom (2:3, 18–19). Believers must resist such teachings, no matter how attractive they might sound. Peter wants his readers to be constantly alert and watchful, testing what they hear against Scripture. If they do not do this, they run the risk of falling from their secure position in Christ (3:17).

Peter ends with an encouragement to his readers to "grow in the grace and knowledge of our Lord and Saviour Jesus Christ" (v. 18). In this way, they will not fall away. Earlier, Peter had told them how they can continue to grow. Firstly, God has given them all the resources they need to live godly and holy lives as they wait for the coming of Jesus (1:3). Secondly, when they make every effort to add one virtue to another—faith, goodness, knowledge, self-control, perseverance, godliness, mutual affection, and love (1:5–7)—they will not stumble and fall from their secure position in Christ.

We can be confident in our security in Christ. But this confidence does not mean that we can live our lives any way we please. New Testament scholar Douglas Moo puts it well when he says: "Confidence in our status with Christ should never lead to a presumption on God's grace that leads us to toy with the danger of false teachers or that negates serious striving after holiness."[16]

We need to be always on our guard, drawing on "his very great and precious promises" (1:4) to enable us to live godly lives while we wait eagerly for the coming of Jesus Christ.

Then, as we come to the close of our study of 2 Peter, we can say together

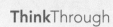

with the apostle: "To him be glory both now and for ever! Amen" (3:18).

[16] Moo, *2 Peter, Jude*, p.213.

What steps can you take to ensure that you will continue to grow in the grace and the knowledge of our Lord and Saviour Jesus Christ?

Which main points or lessons from 2 Peter have struck or inspired you most? Why, and how will you apply them to your life?

Day 22

Read Jude 1:1–2

Jude was the brother of Jesus (see Mark 6:3; Jude is sometimes translated as Judah or Judas). Yet he did not presume upon this relationship to lend weight to his letter. Instead, he identifies himself as "a slave of Jesus Christ" (Jude 1:1, NLT). I prefer this translation to the NIV rendering of "servant", which brings to mind a modern-day servant or domestic helper. That was not what a doulos was in the first century AD. A slave could be bought or sold by his master, had no rights, and owed total allegiance to his master. This was how Jude regarded himself in his relationship with his Lord and Saviour Jesus Christ, as did Paul, Peter, and Jesus' brother James (Romans 1:1; 2 Peter 1:1; James 1:1 NLT). This was the basis of Jude's authority to write this letter.

Jude does not tell us the geographical location of his readers. Instead, he uses three phrases to describe them:

Firstly, they are called (Jude 1:1). God has called them to Himself, to be His holy people (see Romans 1:7). The call was God's initiative, and they responded.

Secondly, Jude's readers are loved in God the Father (Jude 1:1). This speaks of the intimate love that Christians experience in their relationship with God. In New Testament scholar Richard Bauckham's words: "Those whom God loves are taken into the intimate fellowship of God's love, embraced and enfolded by his love. To be in God's love is to be 'in God'."[17] God is the Father and we are His dearly loved children (Ephesians 5:1).

Thirdly, Christians are "kept for Jesus Christ" (Jude 1:1). **God the Father protects His children and keeps them safe for Jesus.** Paul says something similar in 1 Thessalonians 5:23: "May your whole spirit, soul and body be kept blameless at the coming of our Lord Jesus Christ." This is in keeping with Jude's purpose for writing this letter—to warn his readers about the false teachers who have secretly slipped into their midst and are teaching heresies. Jude is confident that God is able to keep them from stumbling (Jude 1:24). However, while they are being kept for Jesus, they too must do their part to keep themselves in God's love as they wait for the coming of Jesus (v. 21).

Before launching into his attack on the false teachers, Jude reassures his readers through his opening greetings that God has called them, loves them, and preserves them for Christ.

[17] Bauckham, *Jude–2 Peter*, p.26.

ThinkThrough

Jude sees himself as a slave of Jesus Christ. What does this tell us about his relationship with Christ? How would you describe your own relationship with Jesus?

Reflect on Romans 6:22. What implications does being "slaves of God" have for the way you live your life?

Take some time to meditate on the fact that we are called, loved in God the Father, and kept for Christ. What encouragement can you find from this amazing truth for your Christian life?

Day 23

Immediately after greeting his readers, Jude goes straight into his reason for writing his letter (Jude 1:3–4). He had originally intended to write about God rescuing them from sin and death through Jesus the Messiah, who died for them and rose again on the third day (v. 3). But he received news that caused him to change his purpose. So, instead of writing about the salvation that he and his readers share, Jude writes to encourage his readers "to contend for the faith that was once for all entrusted to God's holy people" (v. 3).

The reason for his urgent message (and I hope you can sense his urgency) is the stealthy infiltration of certain people into the believers' midst (v. 4). These people mingle with everyone, hiding their true identity and their purpose for being there. Jude is determined to expose them for who they are and for the danger they pose to Christians. **The first step in contending for the faith is to recognise who the enemies are and their tactics.**

Jude does not mince his words: these are ungodly people (v. 4). He uses the word "ungodly" six times in this brief letter (vv. 8, 15, 18). These are people who have rejected God and His authority in their lives (v. 4). And this is clearly seen in their sinful and irreverent acts. They distort the grace of God and use it to justify their sinful lifestyle in sexual immorality, drunkenness, depraved behaviour, and so on (vv. 4, 7, 8, 16). They might have said to Christians: "God loves you and Jesus has died for all your sins. He has set you free. It does not matter what you do with your body. God's grace will cover your sins."

By perverting God's grace and indulging in their immoral lifestyle, these ungodly people are in fact denying "Jesus Christ our only Sovereign and Lord" (v. 4). They reject the authority of Jesus Christ, the only Lord and Master, and turn away from His ethical demands on their lives.

For Jude, there is only one end for these ungodly people: they will stand under God's condemnation (v. 4). This theme of condemnation will make up most of the body of the letter, in which he cites from the Old Testament (vv. 5–8, 11), Jewish works (vv. 9, 14–16), and the teaching of the apostles (vv. 17–18) to support his claim.

So, right from the start, as Jude warns his readers about false teachers in their midst, he also reassures them that these ungodly people will not escape God's judgment. His readers must reject these people and their teachings and way of life. They must continue to acknowledge the authority of Jesus Christ, their only Sovereign and Lord.

ThinkThrough

Have you received or heard teaching that you knew or suspected to be unbiblical? How did you respond?

How can you prepare yourself to "contend for the faith" (Jude 1:3)?

Day 24

Read Jude 1:5–7

Do you recognise the incidents Jude refers to in Jude 1:5–7? These are three examples of people who came under God's judgment in the past. Of the three, you will probably be able to identify two from the Old Testament.

The first is the account of the Israelites who died in the wilderness (Jude 1:5, see Numbers 14). They could not enter the Promised Land because of their unbelief. These Israelites had been miraculously delivered out of Egypt by God, and were sustained by Him during their journey to the Promised Land. But their unbelief brought God's judgment upon them, and they died in the wilderness.

The second Old Testament account you may be familiar with is God's destruction of Sodom and Gomorrah, which had given themselves up to sexual immorality and perversion (Jude 1:7, see Genesis 19). The men of Sodom and Gomorrah demanded to have sex with the two men who were Lot's guests. Presumably, they were already involved in all kinds of sexually immoral conduct including homosexual acts, for Lot's guests— who turned out to be angels— revealed that "the outcry to the LORD against its people is so great that he has sent us to destroy it" (Genesis 19:13).

What about the third example in Jude 1:6, concerning angels who "did not keep their positions of authority but abandoned their proper dwelling"? There is no account of angels sinning and losing their proper dwelling in the Old Testament. However, there was a popular Jewish tradition in Jude's day that these angels were "the sons of God" referred to in Genesis 6:1–4. This is recounted in chapters 6 to 19 of *1 Enoch*, which was part of a collection of books from the period between the Old and New Testaments. These chapters tell of how 200 angels were filled with lust for the beautiful daughters of men on earth and left their proper dwelling in heaven to come down to marry the daughters of men.[18] Their unions produced giants who ravaged the earth, and God judged these angels by casting them into darkness, where they were bound till the last judgment.

All three examples show that God had judged the unbelieving Israelites, the rebellious angels, and the sexually immoral in the past. **God's nature does not change.** So Jude is confident that God will judge the ungodly people who had crept stealthily into the midst of Christians to lure them away from their faith (Jude 1:4). According to

New Testament scholar Douglas Moo, by giving the three examples in this order, "Jude achieves a crescendo in punishment—from physical death (v. 5) to binding in darkness (v. 6) to the 'punishment of eternal fire'" (v. 7).[19]

[18] Please see the study on Day 27 for my comments on *1 Enoch* and the use of extra-biblical sources in the New Testament.
[19] Moo, *2 Peter, Jude*, p.243.

If someone asked, "How can a God of love mete out punishment from physical death to binding in darkness to punishment of eternal fire?", how would you respond?

In 1 Corinthians 10:1–6, Paul says that the things that occurred to the Israelites in the Old Testament serve "as examples to keep us from setting our hearts on evil things as they did". What lessons can you learn from the account of the Israelites wandering in the wilderness (Numbers 13–14)?

Read Jude 1:8–10

Unbelieving Israelites, rebellious angels, and immoral Sodomites—what do these have to do with the false teachers that Jude was warning his readers about? Jude sees similarities between them, in that they are behaving "in the very same way" (Jude 1:8). That is not to say that the false teachers are committing the same sins as the Israelites, the angels, and the people of Sodom and Gomorrah; rather, their sins are of a similar kind.

Jude lists three sins in particular: they "pollute their own bodies, reject authority and heap abuse on celestial beings" (v. 8). He has already written about the first two: the way in which the false teachers have perverted the grace of God and use it to justify their immoral lifestyle (v. 4); and how they have denied Jesus Christ "our only Sovereign and Lord" (v. 4), thus rejecting God's authority in their lives.

What about the third sin of heaping abuse on celestial beings (v. 8)? These celestial beings are angels, who are God's servants and must therefore be treated with respect. The false teachers, however, blaspheme or insult the angels. As they have already rejected the authority of Jesus Christ, it should come as no surprise to us that they would insult God's angels.

By way of example, Jude contrasts their audacity with the restraint of the archangel Michael in the dispute with Satan over the body of Moses (v. 9). This account is not found in the Old Testament, and Jude does not tell us his sources.

Perhaps Jude could be referring to the story of the burial of Moses taken from the Testament of Moses, an early Jewish writing.[20] In this story, the devil accuses Moses of murder and wants to claim Moses' body, but Michael disputes his claim. Instead of condemning the devil for slander, however, Michael refers the matter to the Lord, saying only to Satan, "The Lord rebuke you!" Therefore, Jude argues, no one should say anything bad against angels, even "fallen" ones.

But in insulting or reviling angels, the false teachers are showing how presumptuous and bold they are. They do even what Michael the archangel didn't dare to do. These are matters they do not fully understand, though, ironically, they think they do (v. 10). After all, they claim to be spiritual people because they see visions (v. 9). Jude is very clear that there is only one end for them: destruction (v. 10).

[20] See Bauckham, *Jude-2 Peter*, p.65–76.

ThinkThrough

Some Christians
tend to shy away
from the topic of
God's judgment.
But New Testament
writers like Jude and
Peter speak clearly
about it. Why do you
think God's judg-
ment is an important
matter we should
learn about?

What implications
does God's judg-
ment have for the
way we live our
lives?

Day 26

My husband Philip proposed to me in a letter. I had gone back to Singapore for my summer break while studying in England, and Philip knew that there was someone in Singapore who was not keen on our relationship. So he wrote a three-page proposal letter (there was even a footnote in it!), in which he piled on argument upon argument why I should marry him and not listen to anyone else. He did not want to lose me.

Jude did not want to lose his readers to the false teachers who had stealthily crept into their midst. Perhaps he feels that the three examples from the Old Testament and Jewish tradition (Jude 1:5–7) are not enough, so he cites three more Old Testament examples (v. 11).

The first example is Cain, who murdered his brother Abel (Genesis 4:1–8). Jude is not accusing the false teachers of murder, but is probably referring to Jewish tradition which portrays Cain as "the archetypal sinner and the instructor of others in sin."[21] So Jude warns his readers that the false teachers are following Cain in sinning and teaching others to sin.

The second example is Balaam, whom the king of Moab offered a generous fee to curse Israel (Numbers 22:4–19).

Jewish tradition portrayed Balaam as a man of greed; Jude is implying that the false teachers are profiting financially from their false teaching.

The third example is Korah, who with several others led a rebellion against Moses (Numbers 16:1–14). God judged them by opening up the ground under them, and the earth swallowed them up (vv. 31–33).

Jude applies these three examples to the false teachers, who are portrayed as those who "lead other people into sin."[22] Once again, he makes the point that their sins will not escape God's judgment (Jude 1:13).

In verses 12–13, Jude uses a number of metaphors to reinforce his point about the false teachers: like rainless clouds and fruitless trees, they promise something but do not fulfil them (v. 12). They seem to introduce a life of liberation, but there is only darkness and shame (vv. 12–13). These false teachers eat with the Christians in their love feasts, but show no shame or repentance for their false teaching and immoral lifestyle (v. 12). Jude exposes them for what they are: shepherds who feed only themselves (v. 12).

We must not underestimate the impact of false teachers and their false teachings. **We must learn**

ThinkThrough

to discern truth from error. It is a matter of life and death.

21 Bauckham, *Jude-2 Peter*, p.79.
22 Bauckham, *Jude-2 Peter*, p.79.

There are many people today who reject God's authority and the uniqueness of Jesus Christ. How can you equip yourself to defend against such people and their teachings?

Jude describes the false teachers as "shepherds who feed only themselves" (Jude 1:12). Compare this to what Jesus Christ says about Himself as the good shepherd in John 10:11–18. What can you learn from Him?

Read Jude 1:14–16

Jude's reference to Enoch, "the seventh from Adam", and his prophecy of God's judgment on the false teachers (Jude 1:14–15) might seem puzzling. Certainly, we cannot find an Old Testament prophet named Enoch—but we can find a man called Enoch in Genesis 5:21–24, who was the seventh generation from Adam (see Genesis 5:3–24).

The Jews in the first century AD were familiar with Enoch and a book which was ascribed to him. *1 Enoch* was part of a collection of more than 60 books from the period between the Old and New Testaments, some of which were written in the names of ancient Jewish heroes.[23] The prophecy in Jude 1:14–15 is quite close to 1 Enoch 1:9: "Behold, he will arrive with ten million of the holy ones in order to execute judgment upon all. He will destroy the wicked ones and censure all flesh on account of everything that they have done, that which the sinners and the wicked ones committed against him."[24]

Jude is not the first New Testament writer to cite extra-biblical sources. When Paul addressed the men in the Areopagus in Athens, he also cited writings from the pagan philosopher Aratus (Acts 17:28). Jude could have chosen to quote from *1 Enoch* because he knew that his readers were familiar with this book and regarded it highly.[25] He does not consider *1 Enoch* as Scripture because he does not use the word *graphe* which usually refers to Scripture.[26] He also does not use the usual formula for introducing Old Testament quotations, "as it is written". He uses "prophesied" in verse 14, which refers to the utterance of a prophecy. Clearly Jude agrees with the content of the prophecy regarding the coming of the Lord and His judgment on the ungodly (see Isaiah 66:15; Zechariah 14:5).

Jude could also have chosen this prophecy from *1 Enoch* because of its emphasis on God's judgment on the ungodly; the word "ungodly" appears three times in this prophecy (Jude 1:15). Jude is linking the ungodly people being judged here to the false teachers described in verse 4: when the Lord comes, He will judge them for all their ungodly acts.

God will also judge the false teachers for their ungodly speech (v. 16). They grumble and complain against God; they live to satisfy their own evil desires like sexual lust and greed (see vv. 8, 11); and they speak arrogantly, cosying up to certain people for financial gain.

Jude has gone into great detail to help his readers identify the false teachers in their midst. We, too, need to know the characteristics of false teachers so that we can identify them. **We must not be complacent and accept everything we hear or read, especially from online sources.**

[23] The books are referred to as the *Pseudepigrapha*. *1 Enoch* was written sometime in the first century BC.
[24] As quoted in Moo, *2 Peter, Jude*, p.269.
[25] Moo, *2 Peter, Jude*, p.273.
[26] Moo, *2 Peter, Jude*, p.273.

How do you think you can safeguard yourself from false teaching?

Are you aware of any ungodly acts or words in your life? Ask God to open your eyes to them, ask Him for forgiveness and repent, and take hold of God's promise in 2 Peter 1:3–4.

Day 28

Read Jude 1:17–19

Jude starts the last section of his letter with, "But, dear friends . . ." (Jude 1:17). As you read these words, you might think that he has said enough about the false teachers who had secretly slipped in among the Christians, and is now turning to instruct his readers on how to respond. But that is not the case: Jude has more to say about the false teachers.

They should not be surprised that there are false teachers in their midst, he tells them, for the apostles had specifically foretold that there would be scoffers in the last days. That the false teachers would certainly face God's judgment, too, had been prophesied (vv. 4, 14–15). Jude has exposed their false teachings and their true nature (vv. 4, 8–13); now, he has a few more points to add.

These false teachers care only to satisfy their own ungodly desires (v. 18). They follow their own natural instincts (v. 19), which Jude had earlier likened to that of "irrational animals" (v. 10). Even though these false teachers may consider themselves spiritual, they do not follow the Holy Spirit because they do not have the Spirit in them (v. 19). And if they do not have the Spirit, then they do not belong to Jesus Christ (see Romans 8:8–10).

Furthermore, the false teachers have caused division among the Christians with their erroneous teachings (Jude 1:19). Their very presence in the congregations causes trouble: they participate in the love feasts (v. 12), gather around them those who are eager to listen to their new teaching, and persuade others to join them. But there are also those who reject their false teachings; hence the divisions in the congregations.

All this makes clear that these false teachers do not have the Spirit of God, no matter what they may claim about their own spirituality and dreams (v. 8). **Those who have the Spirit of God will seek to unite Christians, not divide them.**

ThinkThrough

What evidence is there in your life that the Holy Spirit is in you?

Read Ephesians 4:1–3. How can you "make every effort to keep the unity of the Spirit"?

Day 29

Read Jude 1:20–23

I am sure that many people do not really pay attention to the safety procedures explained by airline stewards and stewardesses before a plane takes off. So, in an emergency, some of us may not know what to do if, for instance, the oxygen masks are released. If we had paid attention, we would know that we need to secure our own masks first before helping others. If we don't, we may find ourselves in great danger.

Similarly, Jude encourages his readers to keep themselves in God's love (Jude 1:21) before reaching out to those who may have been influenced by the false teachers. They need to ensure that they are themselves secure first, before they try to help others. How can they do this?

First, the Christians must build themselves up in the faith (v. 20, see also v. 3)—that is, in the teachings of Christ and His apostles. **Only when they are well grounded in their faith, will they be able to withstand and reject false teachings.**

Second, they must pray in the Spirit (v. 20). This means praying prayers that are motivated and guided by the Holy Spirit.

Third, they must keep themselves in God's love (v. 21). Christians are kept

for Jesus Christ (v. 1), who is able to keep them from falling (v. 24). But they must also do their part and remain in God's love. This reminds us of Jesus' words to His disciples in John 15:9: "As the Father has loved me, so have I loved you. Now remain in my love." Jesus goes on to explain that remaining in His love means obeying His commands (v. 10).

Fourth, they must not lose hope, but must look forward to the final expression of Christ's mercy upon His return (v. 21).

All these will help Christians remain secure in Christ. Then they can turn to those who have been influenced by the false teachers. Jude mentions three groups of such people.

There are those who have begun to doubt the teachings of Christ and His apostles (v. 22). These are Christians who have listened to the false teachers and may have been swayed by them. To this group, Jude urges the Christians who have stood firm to be merciful to them, not to rebuke them harshly or reject them.

There are those who are already in the fire (v. 23). If the "fire" here refers to God's judgment, then this group has gone further than the doubters. In New Testament scholar Douglas Moo's words, they "have been

How secure are you in your "most holy faith" (Jude 1:20)?

How can you prepare yourself to help those who have been influenced by false teachings?

tempted to such a degree by the false teachers that they are teetering on the brink of hell."[27] These people must be snatched from the fire before it is too late.

Then there are those whose clothing is stained by corrupted flesh (v. 23). Jude could be thinking of the false teachers themselves or those who have turned from their "most holy faith" (v. 20) to give their allegiance to the false teachers. To this group, Jude urges the Christians to show mercy, for even they are not beyond hope and redemption. But Christians must approach them with fear in case they, too, get lured astray by the false teachers. Secure yourself before helping others!

[27] Moo, *2 Peter, Jude*, p.288.

Day 30

Read Jude 1:24–25

On Day 2, I had shared that I used to be afraid of backsliding, but found reassurance in the fact that God has given us everything we need for life and godliness. These "very great and precious promises" that enable us to overcome sin can be found in 2 Peter 1:3–4. There is another passage which has sustained me in my Christian life: Jude's magnificent doxology in Jude 1:24–25.

Jude praises God because He is the One who is able to keep us "standing upright".[28] While the translation of verse 24 is rendered in many Bible versions as "to keep you from stumbling" (NIV) or "to keep you from falling" (KJV), New Testament scholar Tom Wright argues that the word Jude uses "is a bit more positive: 'to keep you unstumbling'. The image is of someone walking along who might have tripped over, but has not done so in fact."[29] God is able to keep us "standing upright".

Jude is reiterating what he has said at the beginning of his letter, when he described his readers as those "kept for Jesus Christ" (Jude 1:1). So he begins and ends his letter with this wonderful truth: God is able to keep us "unstumbling". But this does not mean that we can live our lives any way we want; we must do our part to keep ourselves in God's love (v. 21).

God seeks to keep us "unstumbling" so that He can present us to himself without fault and with great joy. On the day of judgment, everyone has to stand before God and give an account. For the false teachers, their end is eternal condemnation. But not so for those who reject the false teaching and who continue to grow in the grace and knowledge of our Lord and Saviour Jesus Christ (2 Peter 3:18). For these Christians, God will enable them to appear before His glorious presence without fault—not through their own efforts, but through what Christ had accomplished in His death and resurrection (Jude 1:24). These believers will not dread the day of judgment, because it will be a day of great joy for them. Even in this glorious doxology, Jude is warning against the false teachers who deny Jesus Christ as the only Sovereign and Lord.

Our God is the only God. He is our Saviour. To Him be "glory, majesty, power and authority" (v. 25). These four attributes speak of God's honour and power, and His sovereign rule, both now and forevermore. And all this is mediated "through Jesus Christ our Lord" (v. 25). Jude's doxology reminds us of Paul's doxology in Romans 16:25–27: "To the only wise God be glory for ever through Jesus Christ!"

How apt it is for Jude to end his letter with this magnificent praise to God. What a glorious day that will be, when we are presented without fault and with great joy before the only God our Saviour!

[28] Wright, *Early Christian Letters for Everyone: James, Peter, John and Judah*, p.206.
[29] Wright, *Early Christian Letters for Everyone: James, Peter, John and Judah*, p.206.

ThinkThrough

Are you looking forward to "that day" with eagerness or with trepidation? Why?

Spend some time to ponder on the glory, majesty, power, and authority of God. How will this focus on God's attributes help you in your worship of God and in your daily life?

Journey Through
1 Peter

by David Burge

Why would anyone want to follow Christ when it brings suffering? Does it make sense to hang on to the faith when you might lose your job, or even your own life? The Apostle Peter addresses these questions and more in his first epistle. Journey through 1 Peter, and be inspired by God's grace and His glorious plans for us. Discover the value of pressing on faithfully like His Son, and strengthen your resolve to walk with Jesus through the pains and troubles of this fallen world.

David Burge is a pastor and teaches New Testament at Sydney Missionary and Bible College. His academic interest is in the life and theology of the Apostle Peter, and the ways in which Peter helps us to appreciate Jesus. He has written and published several books, including *2 Peter: Faith in a Sceptical World* and *First-Century Guides to Life and Death: Epictetus, Philo and Peter.*

Journey Through
Romans

by David Cook

The book of Romans outlines what Christians believe and explains God's perfect plan in bringing sinners back to Him. More than any other book in the Bible, it has played a crucial role in shaping church history, and has been called the greatest theological document ever written. Rediscover why the gospel is such good news, and walk away with a deeper appreciation of what and why you believe.

David Cook was Principal of the Sydney Missionary and Bible College for 26 years. He is an accomplished writer and has authored Bible commentaries, books on the Minor Prophets, and several Bible study guides.

Journey Through with your
Bible study group!

Many of our *Journey Through* books now come with group Bible study lessons. All our lessons include printable handouts and lesson plans, which are free for you to use. And several have video contributions as well. Why not *Journey Through* with your Bible study group at **ourdailybread.org/studies**

Browse and purchase all our available *Journey Through* Series books at **ourdailybreadpublishing.org.uk/journey-through**

For information on our resources, visit **ourdailybread.org**. Alternatively, please contact the office nearest you from the list below, or go to **ourdailybread.org/locations** for the complete list of offices.

BELARUS
Our Daily Bread Ministries
PO Box 82, Minsk, Belarus 220107
belarus@odb.org • (375-17) 2854657; (375-29) 9168799

GERMANY
Our Daily Bread Ministries e.V.
Schulstraße 42, 79540 Lörrach
deutsch@odb.org • +49 (0) 7621 9511135

IRELAND
Our Daily Bread Ministries
64 Baggot Street Lower, Dublin 2, D02 XC62
ireland@odb.org • +353 (0) 1676 7315

RUSSIA
MISSION Our Daily Bread
PO Box "Our Daily Bread",
str.Vokzalnaya 2, Smolensk, Russia 214961
russia@odb.org • 8(4812)660849; +7(951)7028049

UKRAINE
Christian Mission Our Daily Bread
PO Box 533, Kiev, Ukraine 01004
ukraine@odb.org • +380964407374; +380632112446

UNITED KINGDOM (Europe Regional Office)
Our Daily Bread Ministries
PO Box 1, Millhead, Carnforth, LA5 9ES
europe@odb.org • +44 (0)15395 64149

ourdailybread.org

Sign up to *Journey Through*

We would love to support you with the *Journey Through* series! Please be aware we can only provide one copy of each future *Journey Through* book per reader (previous books from the series are available to purchase).

If you know of other people who would be interested in this series, we can send you introductory *Journey Through* booklets to pass onto them (which include details on how they can easily sign up for the books themselves).

☐ **I would like to regularly receive the *Journey Through* series**

☐ **Please send me ____ copies of the *Journey Through* introductory booklet**

Just complete and return this sign up form to us at:

Our Daily Bread Ministries, PO Box 1, Millhead, Carnforth, LA5 9ES, United Kingdom

Here at Our Daily Bread Ministries we take your privacy seriously. We will only use this personal information to manage your account, and regularly provide you with *Journey Through* series books and offers of other resources, four ministry update letters each year, and occasional additional mailings with news that's relevant to you. We will also send you ministry updates and details of Our Daily Bread Publishing products by email if you agree to this. In order to do this we share your details with our UK-based mailing house and Our Daily Bread Ministries in the US. We do not sell or share personal information with anyone for marketing purposes.

Please do not complete and sign this form for anyone but yourself. You do not need to complete this form if you already receive regular copies of *Journey Through* from us.

Full Name (Mr/Mrs/Miss/Ms): _____

Address: _____

_____

Postcode: _____ Tel: _____

Email: _____
☐ I would like to receive email updates and details of Our Daily Bread Publishing products.

Signature: _____

All our resources, including *Journey Through*, are available without cost. Many people, making even the smallest of donations, enable Our Daily Bread Ministries to reach others with the life-changing wisdom of the Bible. We are not funded or endowed by any group or denomination.